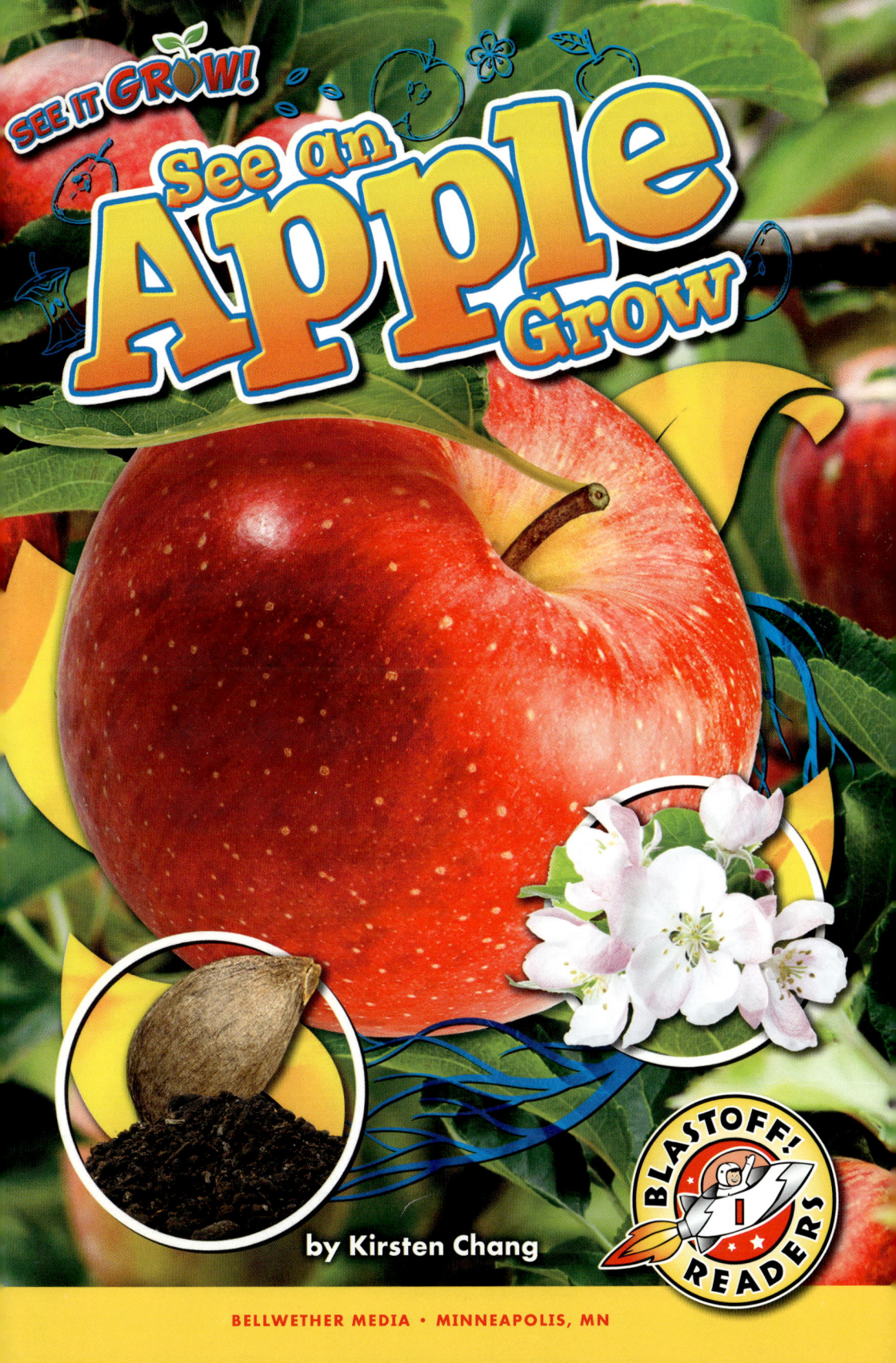

Blastoff! Readers are carefully developed by literacy experts to build reading stamina and move students toward fluency by combining standards-based content with developmentally appropriate text.

 **Level 1** provides the most support through repetition of high-frequency words, light text, predictable sentence patterns, and strong visual support.

 **Level 2** offers early readers a bit more challenge through varied sentences, increased text load, and text-supportive special features.

 **Level 3** advances early-fluent readers toward fluency through increased text load, less reliance on photos, advancing concepts, longer sentences, and more complex special features.

★ Blastoff! Universe

This edition first published in 2024 by Bellwether Media, Inc.

No part of this publication may be reproduced in whole or in part without written permission of the publisher. For information regarding permission, write to Bellwether Media, Inc., Attention: Permissions Department, 6012 Blue Circle Drive, Minnetonka, MN 55343.

Library of Congress Cataloging-in-Publication Data

LC record for See an Apple Grow available at: https://lccn.loc.gov/2023039889

Text copyright © 2024 by Bellwether Media, Inc. BLASTOFF! READERS and associated logos are trademarks and/or registered trademarks of Bellwether Media, Inc.

Editor: Rachael Barnes   Designer: Brittany McIntosh

Printed in the United States of America, North Mankato, MN.

Table of Contents

Round Fruit	4
How Do They Grow?	6
Fully Grown	16
Glossary	22
To Learn More	23
Index	24

Round Fruit

Apples are round, juicy fruits. They grow on trees.

How Do They Grow?

An apple starts as a seed. The seed grows roots in soil.

The seed **sprouts**. It grows into a **seedling**.

seedling

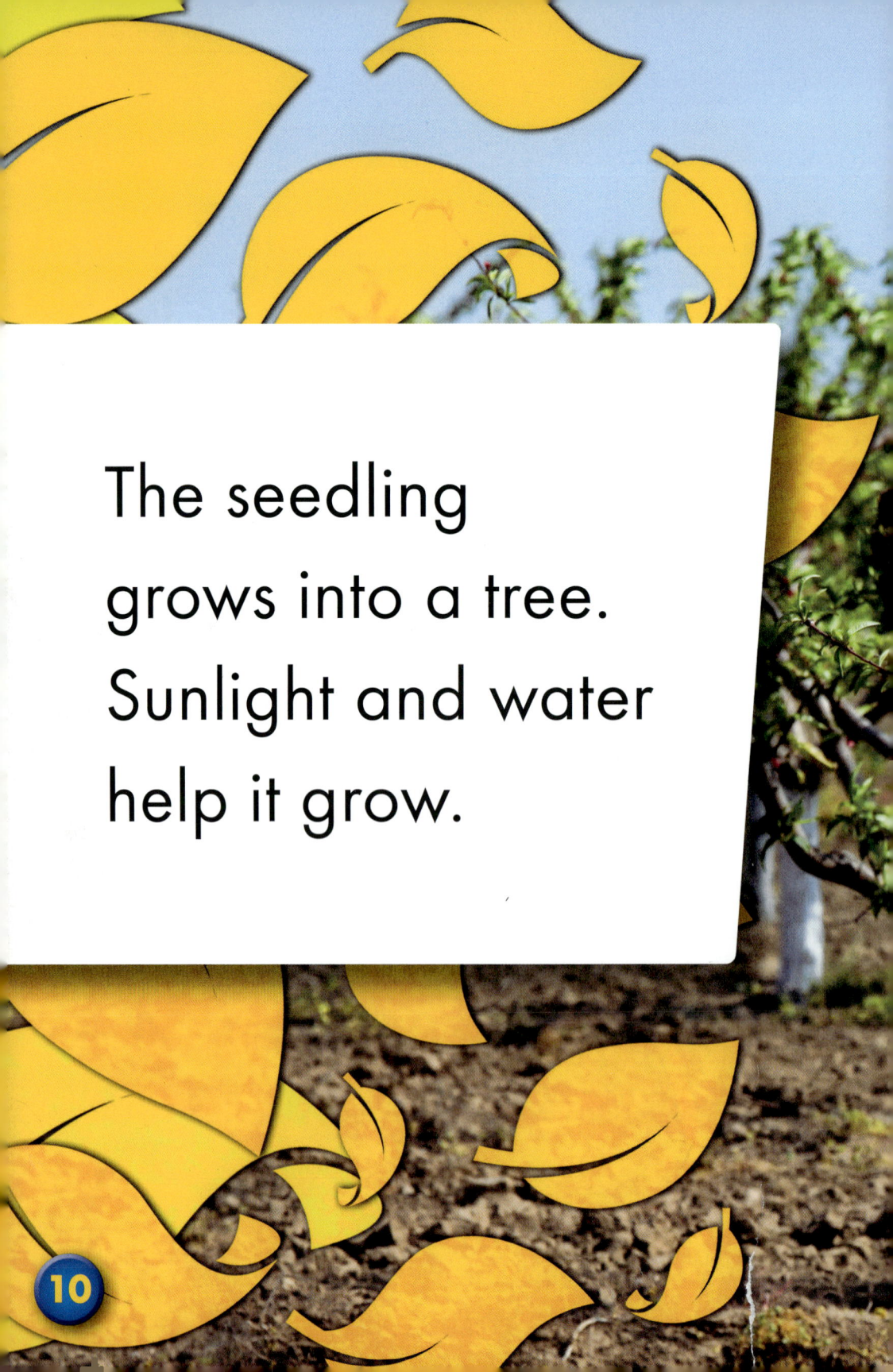

The seedling grows into a tree. Sunlight and water help it grow.

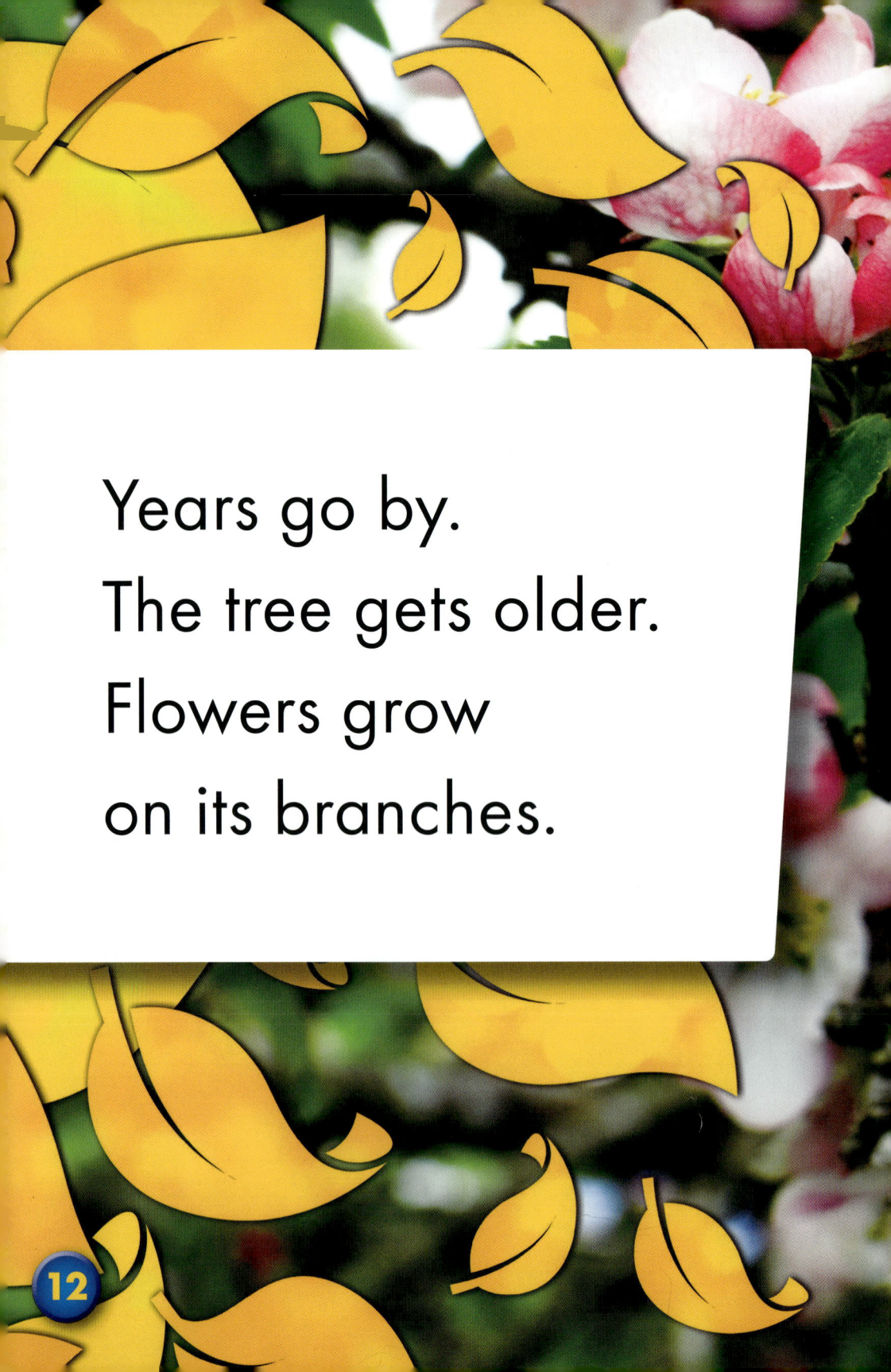

Years go by.
The tree gets older.
Flowers grow
on its branches.

Bees **pollinate** the flowers. Each flower becomes an apple.

bee pollinating a flower

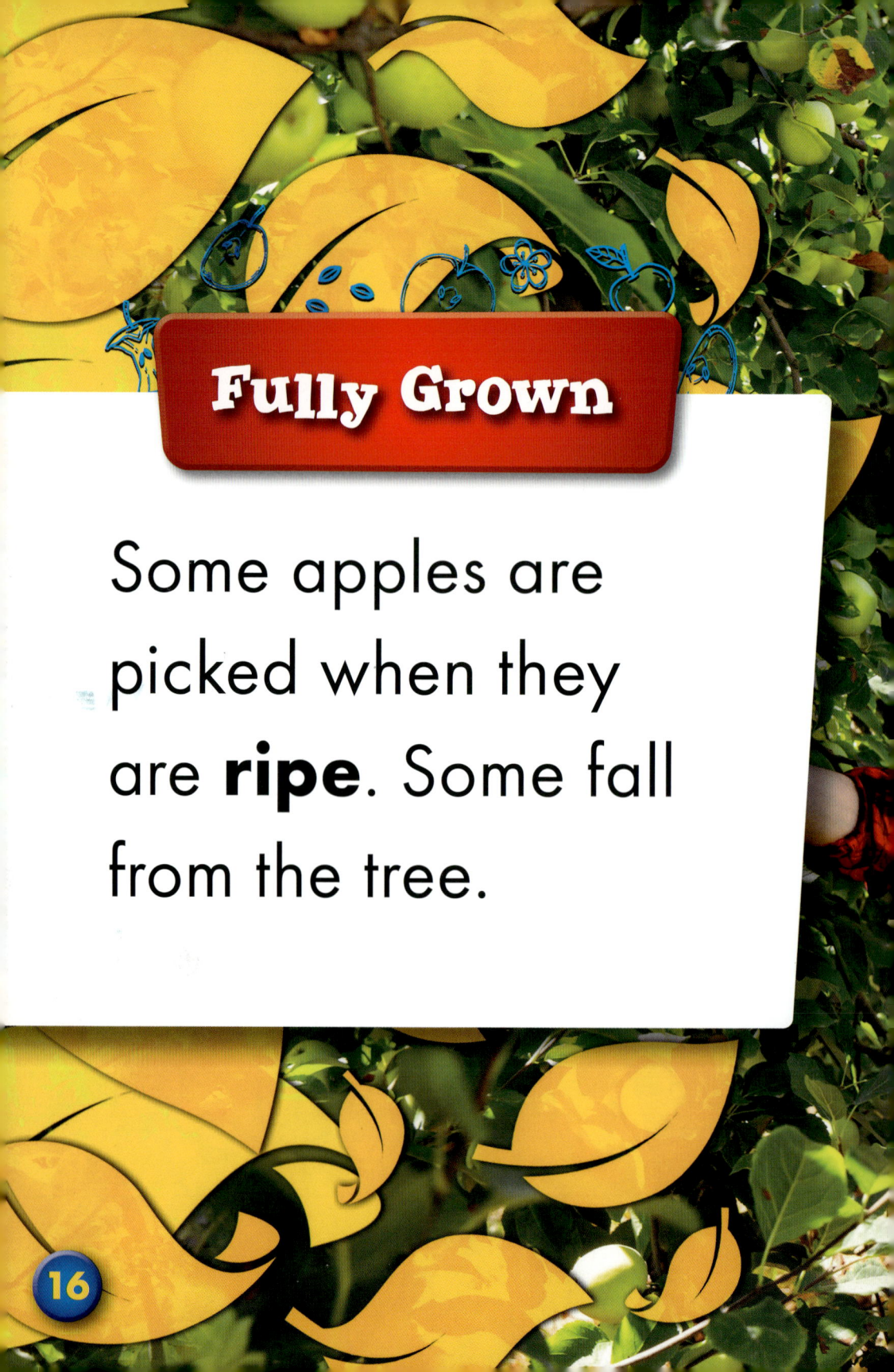

Fully Grown

Some apples are picked when they are **ripe**. Some fall from the tree.

Apples have seeds inside the **core**. Seeds can grow new apple trees!

Apple Life Cycle

1. seeds grow roots
2. seedlings grow into trees
3. trees grow flowers
4. apples grow

core

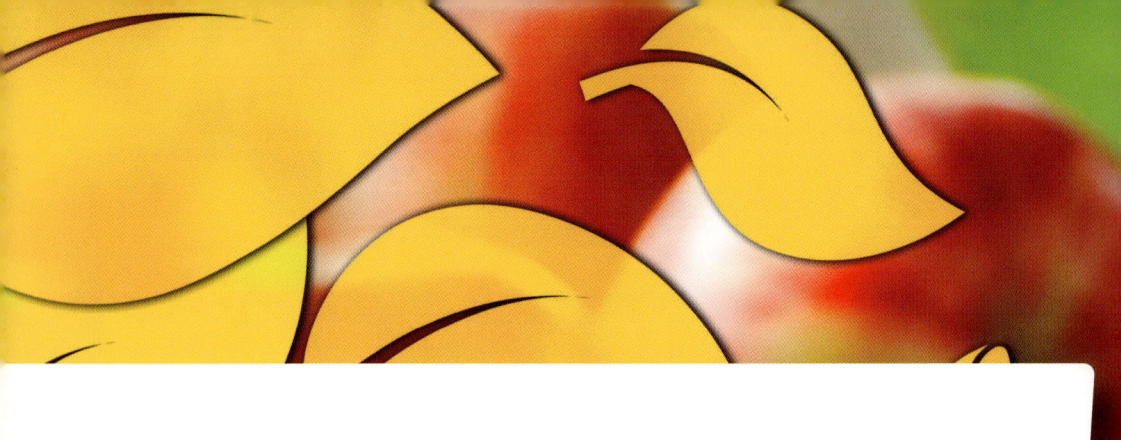

Apples are baked into pies. They are pressed to make juice. Apples make sweet treats!

Using Apples

apple pie · apple juice · applesauce

apple pie

Glossary

core
the center of an apple

seedling
a young apple tree

pollinate
to move a dust called pollen to make seeds grow

sprouts
begins to grow above the ground

ripe
fully grown

To Learn More

AT THE LIBRARY

Ridley, Sarah. *Blossom to Apple*. New York, N.Y.: Crabtree Publishing Company, 2019.

Shepherd, Jodie. *Seed to Apple*. New York, N.Y.: Scholastic, 2021.

Sterling, Charlie W. *Apple*. Minneapolis, Minn.: Jump!, 2023.

ON THE WEB

FACTSURFER

Factsurfer.com gives you a safe, fun way to find more information.

1. Go to www.factsurfer.com.

2. Enter "see an apple grow" into the search box and click 🔍.

3. Select your book cover to see a list of related content.

Index

bees, 14, 15
branches, 12
core, 18, 19
fall, 16
flowers, 12, 13, 14, 15
fruits, 4
juice, 20
life cycle, 19
needed to grow, 11
picked, 16
pies, 20, 21
pollinate, 14, 15
ripe, 16
roots, 6

seed, 6, 7, 8, 18
seedling, 8, 9, 10
soil, 6
sprouts, 8
sunlight, 10
treats, 20
trees, 4, 10, 12, 16, 18
using apples, 21
water, 10

The images in this book are reproduced through the courtesy of: MERCURY studio, front cover (apple); Nella, front cover (flowers); AGCuesta, front cover (seed); grey_and, p. 3; Jules_Kitano, pp. 4-5; Elfe 360, pp. 6-7; S.O.E., pp. 8-9; Edwin Remsberg/ Alamy, p. 9 (inset); Oleksandr Katrusha, pp. 10-11; Nik Merkulov, p. 11 (soil); Cobalt88, p. 11 (sun); Fotokostic, p. 11 (water); AntiD, pp. 12-13; Sodel Vladyslav, pp. 14-15; Petr Bonek, p. 15 (inset); BearFotos, pp. 16-17; Markus Mainka, pp. 18-19; Lesya Dolyuk, pp. 20-21; etorres, p. 21 (apple pie); den781, p. 21 (apple juice); Moving Movement, p. 21 (applesauce); Daxiao Productions, p. 22 (core); pixelnest, p. 22 (pollinate); Serhii Hrebeniuk, p. 22 (ripe); Martin Gstoehl, p. 22 (seedling); Igor Shikov, p. 22 (sprouts); LiliGraphie, p. 23.